CALLS OF THE WILD
NIGHTTIME ANIMALS

WHO'S MAKING THOSE SOUNDS IN THE DARK?

Find out, as you listen to nighttime animals from around the world. In this book you'll meet 15 different animals from six continents. All of them are **nocturnal**, or awake and active at night, when humans and other daytime creatures are asleep.

Just as different animals live in all the habitats around the world, different **species** forage and hunt during all the hours around the clock. Nocturnal animals make their living in the dark. For some, like the kakapo, the darkness gives protection from predators. For some, like the pygmy slow loris, foraging at night means less competition for food. And others, hunters like foxes and owls, come out at night because that's when their prey is awake.

When you turn the page, you'll start your sound safari and meet animals from around the globe, from the Americas, through Australia, Asia, and Europe, all the way to Africa. In each place you'll meet the animals that live in the dark, and you'll hear the nighttime calls of the wild.

Table of Contents

you read, watch for words in **bold**. If they're new to you, you can
what they mean in the handy glossary at the back of the book.

Gray wolves live in the northern parts of the Northern Hemisphere, in areas without many humans. The biggest numbers of wolves live in Alaska, Canada, and northern Asia.

GRAY WOLF

Scientific name: *Canis lupus*

As dusk falls over the forest, the howl of a gray wolf echoes out among the trees. A second wolf joins in, then another, and another, until a singing chorus fills the air. Wolves like to howl together. It strengthens the bonds between members of the **pack**. It's also the way wolves communicate over long distances. If a wolf is away from the group, the pack can howl to say, "Here we are!" When another pack is nearby, the group howls to say, "This is our territory. Keep out!"

Running with the Pack

Gray wolves live and hunt together in packs. A pack can have as few as two or as many as 20 members or more. The pack is usually made up of a breeding pair, called the alpha pair, and their offspring. The group works together to hunt large animals like deer, caribou, and moose. They can roam many miles in search of **prey**.

Top Dog

Gray wolves are the biggest **canids**, or members of the dog family. In fact, this howling hunter is also the ancestor of all **domestic** dogs.

A wolf can eat as much as 20 pounds of meat in one meal!

Great horned owls live nearly everywhere in North America, as well as across much of South America.

GREAT HORNED OWL

Scientific name: *Bubo virginianus*

Who-who-who's there? A great horned owl! This nocturnal hunter's hoots can be heard for miles on a quiet night. Along with their well-known hoots, great horned owls can also squawk, chitter, hiss, squeak, and even make a sound like a low-pitched meow! The one sound owls *don't* make is the sound of flapping wings. Special fringes on an owl's main wing feathers break up noisy air turbulence, so it can swoop down completely silently on its unsuspecting prey.

Feathered Predators

These large birds of prey make their homes in almost every habitat, from forests and deserts to farmland and cities. Great horned owls are fierce hunters. Their prey depends on where they live, but they will eat any animal they can catch, including rodents, rabbits, birds, reptiles, and even frogs and fish.

Owls eat their whole prey. Later, the owl coughs up a pellet of hair, bones, feathers, and other parts that can't be digested.

Nighttime Senses

Great horned owls are built for nighttime hunting. They have huge eyes for spotting prey in the dark. They also have super-sharp hearing. The disklike ruff of feathers on the owl's face acts like a radar dish to channel the sounds of scurrying prey to its ears.

These tree-dwelling frogs live all over the eastern half of the United States and southeastern Canada.

GRAY TREE FROG

Scientific name: *Hyla versicolor* (eastern gray tree frog)
or *Hyla chrysoscelis* (Cope's gray tree frog)

On damp spring and summer nights, male gray tree frogs sing out to their mates with trilling calls. When a gray tree frog sings, he inflates the bubblelike throat sac under his chin. Females don't have throat sacs, so they don't sing. Like crickets, gray tree frogs trill more slowly when the weather is cool and more quickly when it's warm.

Gray? Well . . .

Gray tree frogs are, well, gray. Except when they're brown. Or green. These frogs change color to match their surroundings. A frog may be gray on a dark tree trunk, but it will turn brown or green when it's on the grass or leaves. Their color also changes with temperature. The warmer the weather, the lighter the frog.

Gray tree frogs can survive the winter partially frozen. Their bodies produce a chemical called glycerol, which acts like antifreeze in their blood.

Sticky Climbers

The large, sticky pads at the ends of their toes make it easy for these frogs to climb trees and bushes in the forests where they live. Gray tree frogs spend much of the year hidden among the branches and undergrowth, hunting insects, spiders, and other small animals. But in the spring and summer the males can be found singing around ponds and wetlands.

Snowy tree crickets are found in North America, but there are hundreds of different cricket species all over the world. Each has its own set of songs.

SNOWY TREE CRICKET

Scientific name: *Oecanthus fultoni*

On warm summer nights, crickets sing out in a chirping chorus. Only male crickets chirp. They have different songs for different purposes. The calling song is for attracting mates. The fighting song is for contests between males. Crickets recognize each other by their chirps.

Crickets' ears are on their front legs!

Scrape, Scrape, Chirp!

Crickets chirp by rubbing their front wings together. When the wings rub against each other, a hard ridge on the edge of the left wing scrapes across a row of toothlike pegs on the bottom of the right one. That makes the chirping sound. It's a bit like scraping your thumbnail across the teeth of a comb.

Chirp-o-mometer

Crickets are related to katydids and grasshoppers, and, like all insects, crickets are **ectothermic**, or cold-blooded. They don't create their own body heat, so their bodies are the same temperature as the air around them. A cold cricket has less energy than a warm one, and it chirps more slowly. You can use the chirps of the snowy tree cricket as a thermometer. Using a watch, count the number of chirps in 15 seconds, then add 40. The answer will be close to the temperature in degrees Fahrenheit.

5

A hunting fox sneaks up on its prey, then pounces, almost like a cat.

These medium-size hunters can be found nearly everywhere in the Northern Hemisphere. They live in more parts of the world than any other wild canid.

RED FOX

Scientific name: *Vulpes vulpes*

An eerie, screamlike sound comes from the tall grass at the edge of a farmer's field. A red fox is on the prowl. Along with the "fox scream," red foxes make many other sounds. Their calls have names like the bark, yell-bark, yodel-bark, and "wow-wow" bark, which sounds like a hooting owl. Red foxes also yip, whine, whimper, and cough. When two foxes fight, they make a noise called **gekkering**, which sounds just like its name.

City Slickers

Red foxes make their homes in all kinds of environments, including tundra, deserts, forests, grasslands, farms, suburbs, and even cities. They prefer to live and hunt in places with a mix of habitats, such as forests with clearings and meadows, or the edges of farms and towns.

Fox Food

Red foxes usually hunt small animals like rabbits, squirrels, birds, frogs, or even worms and insects. Red foxes also eat **carrion** (dead animals), fruit, and plants. In areas shared with humans, foxes can be a nuisance when they look for easy meals in people's garbage or prey on chickens or other domestic animals.

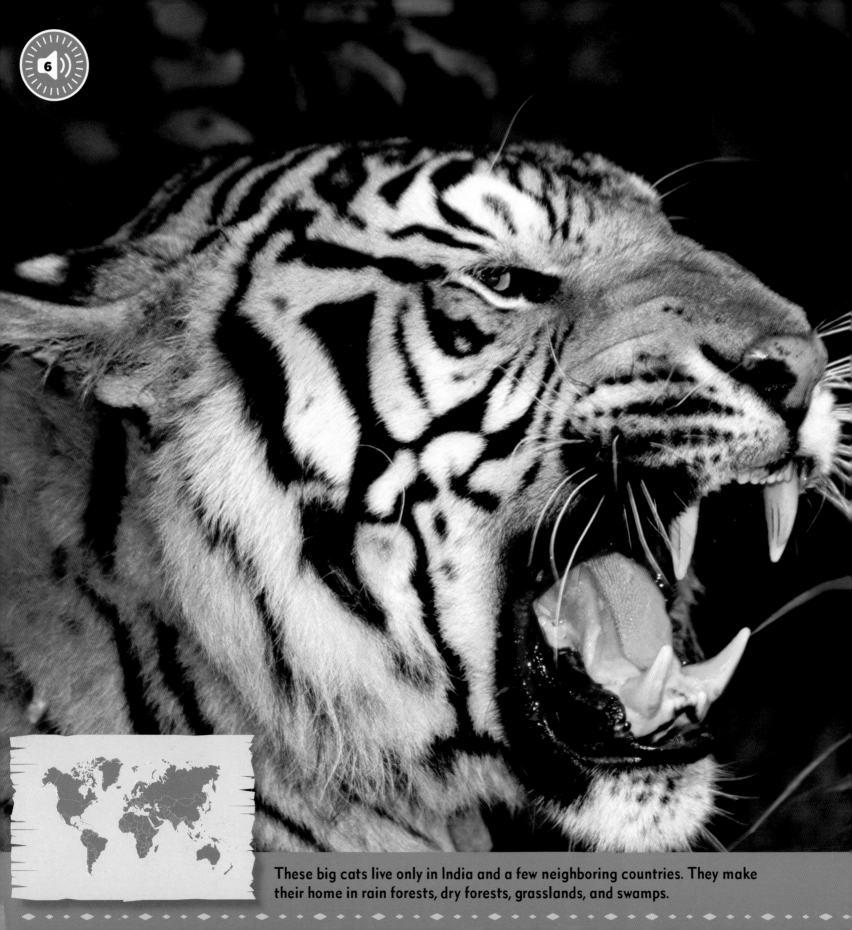

These big cats live only in India and a few neighboring countries. They make their home in rain forests, dry forests, grasslands, and swamps.

BENGAL TIGER

Scientific name: *Panthera tigris tigris*

A deep roar shakes the air as a Bengal tiger announces its kill. Roaring is the loudest sound a tiger makes. It says, "Here I am!" in a voice heard as far as two miles away. Tigers can also snarl, growl, moan, hiss, grunt, and even meow, but they don't purr! Instead, a tiger blows air out through its nose and lips to make a noise called chuffing. It's a friendly greeting between tigers.

Big Cats

These hunters are the second-largest members of the cat family. Only Siberian tigers are bigger. Nose to tail, Bengal tigers can be as long as 9.5 feet and weigh as much as 500 pounds. Their striped coats are perfect camouflage as they stalk their prey from trees or tall grass at night.

Endangered!

Bengal tigers are the most common type of tiger, but there aren't many wild tigers of *any* type left: fewer than 4,000. Tiger hunting is illegal everywhere in the world, but habitat destruction and poaching still threaten them with extinction.

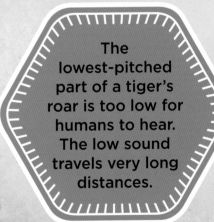

The lowest-pitched part of a tiger's roar is too low for humans to hear. The low sound travels very long distances.

Spotted hyenas live throughout Africa south of the Sahara, except in rain forest and desert areas.

SPOTTED HYENA

Scientific name: *Crocuta crocuta*

What's so funny? It sounds almost like a human giggling, but that doesn't mean anything's funny. When a spotted hyena giggles, it's telling a higher-ranking hyena, "I give up. You're the boss." They also call to each other with loud whoops. Each hyena's whoop is like its individual voice. Hyenas can recognize each other by their whoops from as far as two miles away.

Sticking Together

They live together in groups called **clans**. A clan may have just a few members or as many as 80 or more. The leader of the clan is a female, and all the females in the clan are dominant over the males.

Hyenas look a bit like dogs, but they're really more closely related to cats.

Skillful Hunters

Hyenas once had a reputation as cowardly scavengers who ate the leftover kills of other **predators**. They will eat other animals' kills, even chasing lions away from their own meals, but hyenas are also skillful hunters. The clan breaks up into small groups to hunt, and when they kill a large animal, such as a zebra, the whooping hunters call the rest of the clan to join them in the feast.

Gray-headed flying foxes live on the southeast coast of Australia.

GRAY-HEADED FLYING FOX

Scientific name: *Pteropus poliocephalus*

High in a stand of Australian eucalyptus trees, thousands of giant bats chatter, chirp, and squawk. It's a flying fox camp, where these fruit- and nectar-eating bats hang by their feet to roost during the day. Now it's dusk, and they're heading out to forage. Flying foxes can travel as far as 20 or 30 miles to reach their feeding grounds each night. They return to the camp at dawn.

What Do You Hear?

Unlike insect-eating bats, flying foxes don't use **echolocation** (sound waves) to navigate and find food. Instead, they use their eyes and noses. While the high-pitched sounds of insect-eating bats are out of our hearing range, the squeaks and chatters of gray-headed flying foxes can easily be heard by humans.

These bats have a 3-foot wingspan and weigh as much as 2 pounds.

Cozy Campers

Flying fox camps range in size from a few hundred bats to tens of thousands. Gray-headed flying foxes can migrate as far as 450 miles between summer and winter habitats. They return to the same camps year after year. Most have been in use for more than 100 years. Gray-headed flying foxes often share their camps with another species, the black-headed flying fox.

Pygmy slow lorises live in the rain forests of Vietnam, Cambodia, Laos, and southern China.

PYGMY SLOW LORIS

Scientific name: *Nycticebus pygmaeus*

What are those chittering trills, whistles, and clicks? A group of pygmy slow lorises! Only 8 inches long and weighing less than a pound, these tree dwellers have strong hands and feet for gripping, and often hang from branches by their feet while using their hands to hold food. Although they crawl very slowly among the branches, their hands can dart out quickly to catch beetles or other insects.

Dangerously Cute!

Slow lorises may look cute, but they can be dangerous. Glands on the inside of their elbows produce a strong-smelling oil. When the oil mixes with saliva in a loris's mouth, it creates a powerful venom. A slow loris bite can cause a severe allergic reaction or even death—just one of the reasons these wild animals do *not* make good pets.

A pygmy slow loris sleeps in tree holes or dense branches during the day, curling up into a ball with its head tucked between its legs.

The Better to See You With

Big eyes with big pupils let in more light, and nocturnal animals' eyes are usually bigger for their body size than the eyes of **diurnal** (daytime) animals. Like many nighttime animals, lorises have a reflective layer at the back of their eyes to reflect and amplify light.

Striped skunks can squirt their spray up to 20 feet.

Striped skunks can be found throughout most of North America, from the southern half of Canada all the way to northern Mexico.

STRIPED SKUNK

Scientific name: *Mephitis mephitis*

You might hear them rustling through the undergrowth at night, but more often it's the smell that hits you first. That's because striped skunks don't often make sounds with their voices. When they do, it's usually because they're startled. They also use their voices to communicate with other skunks. Striped skunks make churring and growling sounds, coo and twitter like birds, hiss, shriek, and squeal.

Tasty Treats

Skunks are **omnivores**—they eat both animals and plants. Their food is mostly insects such as grasshoppers, crickets, beetles, and caterpillars. They also eat bigger animals like mice and young birds, along with fruit, corn, and other plants.

Spray It, Don't Say It!

These cat-sized mammals don't smell bad themselves. It's only their defensive spray that stinks. If a skunk is startled or cornered by a predator or other animal (or human!), it will arch its back, raise its tail, stamp on the ground with its front feet, and shuffle quickly backward. That's the signal to back off! If the intruder doesn't retreat, the skunk twists around, raises its tail, and sprays its enemy with blinding, awful-smelling musk.

Hedgehogs hunt by smell and hearing. They don't have very good eyesight.

European hedgehogs live throughout most of Europe except for the far north.

EUROPEAN HEDGEHOG

Scientific name: *Erinaceus europaeus*

Hedgehogs get their name from their tiny, piglike snouts and the way they root through hedges and undergrowth. They snuffle and grunt like tiny pigs while foraging for the insects and other animals they eat. Hedgehogs also snort and hiss when startled or annoyed. They grow to be as long as 12 inches and weigh between 1 and 2 pounds, depending on the time of year. They fatten themselves up in the fall when they are preparing to hibernate for the coming winter.

Spiny Foragers

Hedgehogs eat mostly insects, worms, and other **invertebrates**, or animals without backbones. They will also eat small **vertebrates** (animals with backbones) such as frogs and young mice. Hedgehogs eat some plants, too, but plants aren't a large part of their diet. These prickly animals help gardeners by eating pest insects, snails, and slugs.

Prickly Pigs

Hedgehogs protect themselves from predators by curling into a ball with their prickly spines sticking out. They sleep in the same position. A hedgehog has around 5,000 spines. The hedgehog makes them stand up using a layer of muscles under its skin. In spite of the spines, predators like badgers, foxes, and owls manage to prey on hedgehogs.

With a life span of up to 90 years, kakapos are one of the longest-living birds on earth.

Kakapos live only in New Zealand.

KAKAPO

Scientific name *Strigops habroptilus*

A booming call, like short blasts on a foghorn, rings out for miles through the forest. It's the call of a male kakapo, one of the rarest animals in the world. During breeding season, male kakapos gather at an area of the forest called a **lek**. At the lek, each bird digs a shallow, bowl-shaped depression in the ground. He sits in this bowl and booms in hopes of attracting a female. Females and males also screech like other members of the parrot family.

Big Birds

Kakapos are the world's heaviest parrots, weighing in at as much as 9 pounds. They have powerful legs for walking and tree-climbing, but their wings are only good for balancing, or to slow their fall when jumping out of trees. Kakapos eat fruit, seeds, stems, roots, bark, and other parts of plants.

Back from the Brink

There are only around 125 living kakapos in the world today. But that number is up from 20 years ago, when there were just 50 of these parrots left. Nonnative mammal predators had hunted them almost to extinction. In an effort to save them, all the wild kakapos were moved to small islands with no mammals.

Raccoons make their dens in places like tree holes, hollow logs, and even people's attics.

Raccoons' masks and ringed tails are a common sight in much of North America, from southern Canada all the way south to Central America.

RACCOON

Scientific name: *Procyon lotor*

Raccoons churr, purr, growl, snort, grunt, cry, whistle, screech, and chitter. The different calls have different meanings. Startled raccoons whistle. When attacked, they screech in alarm. Growls and grunts are warnings to stay away. Purring, churring, and chittering are all ways that mother raccoons communicate with their young.

Curious Bandits

As omnivores, raccoons eat both plants and animals, and are successful city dwellers. They are curious, smart, and good at solving problems such as breaking into "raccoon-proof" garbage cans in search of food.

Handy Paws

Raccoons use their sensitive and nimble front paws to handle food and other objects. Because they often rub their food between their paws and also use them to dabble in the water, the legend arose that raccoons wash their food before eating it. But raccoons rub their food even when there's no water around, and they often dip their paws in the water just to search for crayfish or other tasty animals.

A Tasmanian devil can eat more than a third of its own weight in one meal.

Tasmanian devils live only on the Australian island of Tasmania.

TASMANIAN DEVIL

Scientific name: *Sarcophilus harrisii*

A growling, shrieking ruckus breaks out in the Australian bush. It's a group of Tasmanian devils, squabbling as they feast on a carcass. These bulldog-sized predators are both hunters and scavengers. They are famously fierce and can bring down prey like wallabies or wombats twice their size. Devils hunt and scavenge on their own, but they gather in groups to feed. Their competition for places at the carcass is noisy and ferocious, but real fights are rare.

Devilish Behavior

This **marsupial** earned the name "devil" from its fierce attitude and snarling sounds. A Tasmanian devil will growl, snort, cough, hiss, and shriek when attacking or defending itself. The devil's ears turn bright red when it's angry, scared, or excited. A wide-open mouth with needle-sharp teeth usually means the devil is frightened or anxious, not angry.

Little Imps

Like all marsupials, baby Tasmanian devils, known as imps, spend the first part of their lives inside their mother's pouch. Newborn devils are tiny, hairless, and eyeless. After birth they crawl into their mother's pouch and stay there for the next three and a half months. When they emerge, the playful babies have all their fur, and their eyes are open.

Eurasian badgers live throughout Europe as well as in parts of the Middle East.

EURASIAN BADGER

Scientific name: *Meles meles*

Badgers communicate with many different sounds. Threatening or defensive badgers may hiss, snarl, growl, and make a chattering sound called **keckering**. Keckering sounds a little like a red fox's gekkering, but is lower in pitch. A surprised badger may snort or bark. Friendly badgers grunt softly to each other, and cubs chirp, coo, and cluck. Mother badgers purr to gather or encourage their cubs. When separated from its mother, a cub will wail to get her attention.

Sturdy Diggers

European badgers are the size of medium dogs, between 2 and 3 feet long. They are built for digging, with stocky bodies and powerful front legs and claws. Badgers are omnivores, eating both plants and animals. One of their main foods is earthworms, and a badger can eat hundreds of worms in a night. Other badger foods include insects, fruit, grains, and small mammals such as hedgehogs.

Get Sett . . .

Badgers spend two-thirds of their time in underground burrows called setts. The sett is a network of connected tunnels with sleeping chambers, toilet areas, and several entrances. Badgers like to dig their setts with entrances hidden behind rocks, trees, or shrubs. They often line the chambers with dried grass or leaves.

Female badgers are called sows. Males are boars, and babies are called cubs.

GLOSSARY

Canid: a member of the dog family.

Carrion: dead animal carcasses.

Clan: a group that lives and hunts together.

Diurnal: awake and active in the daytime.

Domestic: animals that have been bred to live with humans.

Echolocation: using sound waves to find food and other objects.

Ectothermic: animals that don't make their own body heat.

Gekkering: a chattering, chuckling sound made by some animals.

Invertebrate: an animal without a backbone.

Keckering: a chattering, chuckling sound made by some animals, but which is lower in pitch than gekkering.

Lek: a breeding ground where males of certain species gather together to attract mates.

Marsupial: a mammal whose young stay in a pouch after birth.

Nocturnal: awake and active at night.

Omnivore: an animal that eats both plants and other animals.

Pack: a group of wolves or other members of the dog family that lives and hunts together.

Predator: an animal that hunts and eats other animals.

Prey: the animals that a predator eats.

Species: a group of similar animals, plants, or other living things that can breed together.

Vertebrate: an animal with a backbone.